Together!

by Geoffrey Marshall-Taylor

illustrated by George W. Thompson

Collins

God's world

Lord, thank you for the world you made:
thank you for the life you gave;
thank you for the sky and breeze;
thank you for the plants and trees.

Praise God from whom all blessings flow;
Praise him, all creatures here below.

See the clouds moving across the sky;
Dear God, thank you for your world.
Hear the birds singing on the rooftops;
Dear God, thank you for your world.

All things bright and beautiful,
all creatures great and small,
all things wise and wonderful,
the Lord God made them all.

Each little flower that opens,
each little bird that sings,
he made their glowing colours,
he made their tiny wings.

The purple-headed mountain,
the river running by,
the sunset and the morning,
that brightens up the sky.

The cold wind in the winter,
the pleasant summer sun,
the ripe fruits in the garden,
he made them every one.

He gave us eyes to see them,
and lips that we might tell
how great is God almighty,
who has made all things well.

All things bright and beautiful,
all creatures great and small,
all things wise and wonderful,
the Lord God made them all.

Mrs C.F. Alexander

Heavenly Father,
thank you for all the different things around us.
It would be a dull world
if you had made everything the same.

There are different shapes like these

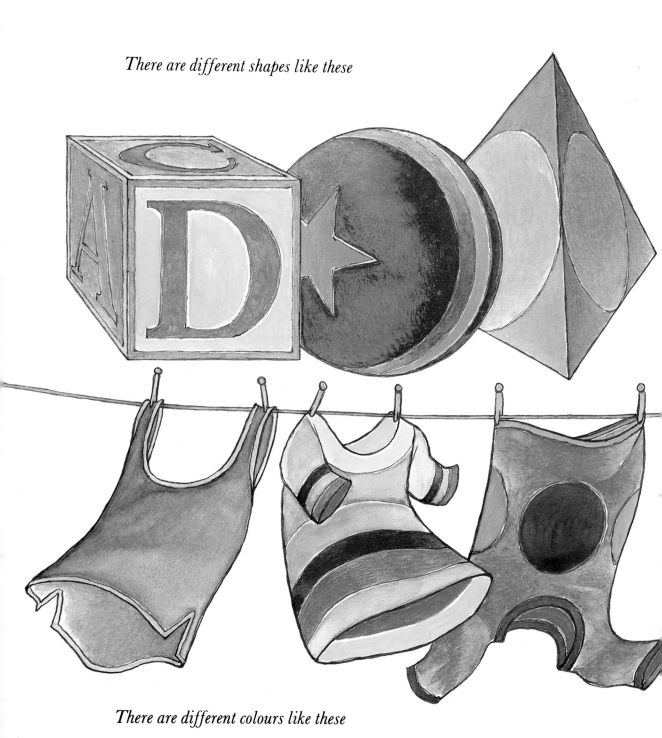

There are different colours like these

There are different sizes like these

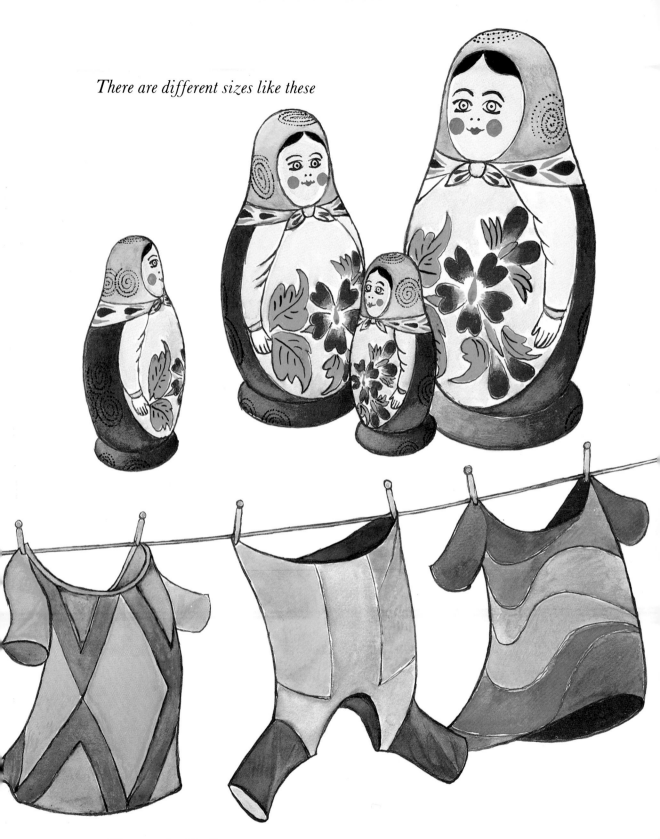

Heavenly Father,
thank you for all the different things around us.

Animals in zoos, in films, in books;
hundreds, thousands with different looks:
the monkey and the kangaroo,
the eagle and the cockatoo;
the tall giraffe, the crawling snail,
the tiny mouse, the giant whale;
the bear, the emu and the gnat,
the crab, the donkey and the bat.
Thank you for them, large and small,
thank you, God, who made them all.

Dear God, help us to look after our pets properly.
Sometimes we're too rough with them;
sometimes we just don't bother about them.
They need food and drink; they need to be warm and clean.
Thank you that they are friendly and give us so much fun.
Help us to look after them properly.

Holy, holy, holy Lord,
God of power and might,
heaven and earth are full of your glory.

Glory be to you, O Lord most high.   Amen.

Sow a seed, and soon you'll see
a tiny flower, a tiny tree;
look at all the plants around,
pushing, growing from the ground.

For potatoes, beans and cabbages,
   Lord, we give you thanks.
For tomatoes, peas and lettuces,
   Lord, we give you thanks.
For apples, plums and raspberries,
   Lord, we give you thanks.
For cherries, pears and strawberries,
   Lord, we give you thanks.

Dear God, some boys and girls are hungry today:
   they haven't any food to eat;
some boys and girls are thirsty today:
   they haven't any water to drink.
We have plenty to eat, so we're sorry that we're greedy.
We have plenty to drink, so we're sorry that we're wasteful.
Help us not to grumble.
Help us to be thankful for our meals. For Jesus' sake.   Amen.

First the farmer sows the seeds,
then God sends the rain they need;
the plants shoot up before too long —
God sends the sun to make them strong.
Praise God for the rain and sun;
praise God for the farmer.

The wheat is ripe: it's harvest time again.
Praise God for the golden grain.

The grain is crushed the flour to make;
we need the flour, when we bake
bread and biscuits, pies and cakes.
Thank you, God, for Jesus' sake.

Thank you for the world so sweet,
thank you for the food we eat,
thank you for the birds that sing,
thank you, God, for everything.

E Rutter Leatham

15

In the country

Cows, horses, chickens, sheep and pigs:
   thank you, Lord, for farm animals;
tractors, trailers, combines, sprays and ploughs:
   thank you, Lord, for farm machinery;
shepherds, tractor drivers, stockmen:
   thank you, Lord, for farm people.

All year round the work goes on,
in winter's cold and summer's heat;
Lord, thank you for the farmers
who grow the food we eat.

In the town

There seem so many people
    who are busy in a town;
in the buses, in the shops,
    or walking up and down.
Lord, I'm sure you love them
    when they laugh and when they cry,
for you even know each sparrow
    as it flies down from the sky.

Dear God, sometimes I want to spend a lot of time looking in toy shops, when other people want to move on. I'm sorry for the times I am fed up and impatient. Please help me to think more about others than about myself. For Jesus' sake.   Amen.

Dear Lord, we have to go shopping tomorrow. It can be very tiring, so please help us not to get cross; it can be hard to choose what to buy, so please help us to spend our money sensibly.
For Jesus' sake.   Amen.

My senses

Thank you, Lord, for eyes to see
the world and all it has for me.
  People here and people there —
  I see their clothes, I see their hair.
  The colour, shape and size I know
  of birds that fly, of plants that grow,
  of boats and books, of chairs and cheese,
  of toys and trains, of pens and peas.
Thank you, Lord, for eyes to see
the world and all it has for me.

Thank you, Lord, for hands to touch:
  smooth things, rough things,
  soft things, hard things,
  warm things, cold things,
  square things, round things,
  short things, long things,
  big things, small things.
Thank you, Lord, for hands to touch.

Thank you, Lord, for everything that smells nice:
   for flowers and grass, bananas and pears,
   for all the food which  prepares.

Say the name of the grown up who got your meals today.

Thank you, Lord, for everything that smells nice.

Lord, thank you for the fun of tasting:
   for soft ice cream and chewy meat,
   for scrunchy crisps and sticky sweets,
   for apples, oranges and plums,
   for bread, biscuits, butter and buns,
   for honey, jam and marmalade,
   for water, milk and lemonade.
Lord, thank you for the fun of tasting.

Lord, if I were deaf and I couldn't hear
sounds from far or sounds from near:
   I wouldn't hear a spoken word,
   a noisy car, a singing bird.
   Records, radio, T.V.
   would all go on, but silently.
   'Goodnight!' 'Look out!' 'Hold hands!' 'Hello!'
   — these are words I would not know.
Thank you, Lord, that I can hear
sounds from far and sounds from near.

Warm times

I love to play in the summer heat;
I love to run in my bare feet;
I love the water in the pool;
I love the drinks that make me cool;
I love the smell of grass and flowers;
I love to stay outside for hours.
Lord, thank you for each sunny day:
thank you for the games I play.

Dear God,
if it's sunny tomorrow we're going out for the day.
Please help us to have a happy time
and keep us safe on the way.

Cold times

It was cold today! What a strange sight:
all the garden was covered with white!
Frost on the grass, frost on the trees;
frost on the soil, frost on the leaves;
frost on the windows, frost on the wall;
frost on the rooftops, frost covers all.
As I sit inside with thick clothes on,
thank you, Lord, that I keep warm.

Snowflakes falling down and down,
settling gently on the ground.
Thank you, Lord: it's so much fun
to play outside in the snow and the sun.

Dear God, please be with old people when it's icy or snowy.
Help them to be safe when they go out and help them to be warm
when they stay in.   For Jesus' sake.   Amen.

Around the world

Dear God, all the people in the world are part of your family. Thank you that you love each man and each woman, each boy and each girl. Help me to love others, whatever they are like, for Jesus' sake.

Lord, in some ways we're different from other people:
  big countries, small countries,
  hot countries, cold countries,
  flat countries, hilly countries,
  rich countries, poor countries.
But, thank you that in many ways we're the same:
  we eat, we drink;
  we smile, we cry;
  we work, we rest;
  we live, we die.
Yes, Lord, in many ways we are the same. Thank you.

Lord, many people in the world live in rickety houses:
the rain drips through the roof and makes them wet;
the wind whistles through the walls and makes them cold;
please take care of them and help them soon to have better houses.
We ask this in Jesus' name.   Amen.

Dear God,
bless the boys and girls who are not as happy as I am:
Some have no families; some have nowhere to live;
some have no toys; some have nowhere to play;
some have no food; some have nowhere to learn.
Dear God,
bless the boys and girls who are not as happy as I am.

Lord, bless the people of
Say the name of a place where there has been a disaster.
Please be with the doctors and nurses
and all those who are trying to help there.
For Jesus' sake.   Amen.

Friends

Dear God, I like being with my friends.
Thank you for the fun we have together.
I'm sorry that sometimes I don't share my toys with them;
I'm sorry that sometimes I try to be bossy with them.
Help me to make them happy while we're playing.

Lord, some of my friends can run faster than I do;
some can draw more neatly than I do;
some can climb higher than I do.
Sometimes I get upset when I'm not as good as they are.
Help me not to worry about it, but to do my best.
For Jesus' sake.   Amen.

Dear God, thank you for the people who make me laugh:
they pull funny faces,
they say funny things,
they make funny noises.
Thank you for the people who make me laugh.

Lord, I sometimes get impatient with my friends,
especially when they're slower or clumsier than I am.
Help me to be patient.   For Jesus' sake.   Amen.

Some boys and girls are lonely,
because they've no one to play with;
Lord, help me to be friends with them,
so that they won't feel left out.

Lord, I know that you will forgive me,
   when I do something wrong:
Please help me to say 'sorry' when I've upset someone else.
Please help me to forgive other people when they upset me.
For Jesus' sake.   Amen.

People who help us

Dear God, be with all the people who work through the night: people in airports and hospitals, power stations and telephone exchanges; doctors, firemen, the ambulance service and the police.
Thank you for them all.   Amen.

Thank you, God, for fishermen
who risk their lives in boats;
when the wind is high and the waves are rough,
please keep them all afloat.
Please bring them safely back to land
with fish for us to eat,
and help their families not to fear,
for soon again they'll meet.

Thank you, Lord,
for the people who served us in the shops today:
it's easy for them to become tired and impatient when they're busy,
so please help us to be polite and helpful to them.
For Jesus' sake.   Amen.

Thank you, Lord,
    for everyone who helps us to enjoy ourselves:
for people who make the television programmes I watch;
for people who produce the records I listen to;
for people who write books and illustrate them;
for people who invent toys and games.
Thank you, Lord,
    for everyone who helps us to enjoy ourselves.

Thank you, God, for the people who look after me.
Thank you especially for
Say the names of the grown ups who live with you.
There's always so much to do:
shopping, painting, cooking, digging,
cleaning, hammering, washing, mending.
They're all jobs which make people very tired.
Thank you, God, for the people who look after me.

Lord, I'm sorry for the times when I'm not very helpful:
   I leave my clothes and toys all over the floor;
   I forget to take off my muddy boots and shoes;
   I spill my drinks and paints on the furniture;
   I make a noise when other people want to be quiet.
Lord, please make me more helpful every day.

Old people and young people

Dear God, I pray for all the old people I know,
especially for   and

Say their names.

If they are lonely or tired or ill,
be close to them;
if they find things hard to do,
help them not to give up.
Through Jesus Christ our Lord.   Amen.

Tiny babies need your care;
Lord, protect them, everywhere.

Thank you, Lord, that   and   have a new baby;

Say the names of the parents and their other children.

please help them all to be happy together;
please help the new baby to grow up to be well and strong.
For Jesus' sake.   Amen.

Sick people

Lord, I'm not well today.
Please help me to feel better tomorrow.
Thank you for  who looks after me.
Say the name of the grown up who is looking after you.

Dear God, my friend 🧍 is sick.
Say the name of your friend who is sick.
Please help *him* to get well quickly.
For Jesus' sake.   Amen.

Lord, thank you for the people who make me better when I'm ill:
for my family and my doctor. Thank you for the medicines I take
and for the chemist who prepares them.

Dear God, please be with ⚲ who has gone into hospital.

Say the name of the person who has gone into hospital.

Please be close to *her* so that *she* doesn't feel lonely;
please help the doctors and nurses to make *her* better quickly;
please bring *her* home again soon. For Jesus' sake.   Amen.

Thank you, Lord, for everyone who looks after sick people,
especially for doctors, nurses and hospital workers.
When they are tired, give them strength;
please help them
to know the best way to make people well again.

35

Me

Lord, when I'm afraid, I need you near me,
Thank you that you'll never leave me.

The King of love my shepherd is,
whose goodness faileth never.
I nothing lack if I am his,
and he is mine for ever.

Sir Henry Baker

Dear God, sometimes I feel lonely. Help me to remember that you are always near me. Help me to remember that I can talk to you at any time. Thank you for being my friend and for listening to me.

When children came to Jesus, some said, 'Go away';
but when Jesus saw the children, he said, 'Come and stay'.
Lord, thank you that you are my friend,
and that your love will never end.   Amen.

Dear God, I sometimes think that no one likes me.
Help me to be sorry, if it's all my fault.
Help me to understand that people can be cross and still love me.
Help me to be kind even when others are unkind to me.
For Jesus' sake.   Amen.

Inside and outside

I like coming home after I've been out.
I like to see my favourite toys and books;
I like to see the rest of my family;
I like to see my own room.
Thank you, God,
  for everything which makes me happy at home.

Lord,
there are all sorts of dangerous things in my house:
I could cut myself on the sharp knives;
I could get an electric shock from the plugs and switches;
I could burn myself with fire.
Please protect me and my friends and my family
from dangers like these.
Help me to be sensible and to take care.

It's nice outside when the rain comes down,
  in my boots and coat I'm dry and warm;
it's nice inside when the rain comes down,
  with my toys and books I'm dry and warm.
Thank you, God.   Amen.

Dear God, it's fun playing outside:
   I like
      the whoosh of the wind as I swish on the swing;
   I like
      the world whizzing round as the roundabout turns;
   I like
      the bump as I jump from the climbing frame bars;
   I like
      to chase and to run in the warmth of the sun;
   I like
      to roll down a slope, to kick a ball high;
   I like
      the tug of the breeze at my kite in the sky;
Dear God, it's fun playing outside.

Music and dancing

I like to sing, I like to shout,
I like to move and dance about.

Thank you for the mouth I use for singing,
thank you for the ears I use for hearing,
thank you for the legs I use for dancing,
thank you for the hands I use for clapping.

God is very good to us
Let's praise him.
Let's play the trumpet
Let's praise him.
Let's play the guitar
Let's praise him.
Let's play the drums
Let's praise him.
Let's play the violins
Let's praise him.
Let's play the recorders
Let's praise him.
Let's crash the cymbals
Let's praise him.
Let's dance for joy
Let's praise him.

A.J. McCallen, *Listen!*
(Psalm 150)

Words

Dear God,
you know that sometimes I say things that I shouldn't:
when I make a promise, help me to keep it;
when I upset someone, help me to say sorry;
when I talk about myself, help me to tell the truth;
when I speak about others, help me to be kind.
For Jesus' sake.   Amen.

Words can be kind, words can be thoughtful,
words can be rude, words can be hurtful,
words can be hard, words can be fun,
Lord, help me, as I use them one by one:
help me to take care and be wise every day
in the way that I speak and the words that I say.

At the start of the day

Father, for another night
of quiet sleep and rest,
for all the joy of morning light,
your holy name be blest.

I wake up in the morning;
I see the new day dawning.
Help me, Lord, until tonight
to do the things I know are right.

Lord, be with me in all I do today;
as I rest and work and eat and play;
Lord, protect me from all wrong
and keep me cheerful all day long.

Lord, please be with Daddy and Mummy while they're working. When they're busy, help them not to be too tired. When they meet other people, help them to get on with them. When things go wrong, help them to be calm. When they're not sure what to do, help them to know what's best.   For Jesus' sake.   Amen.

For this new morning with its light,
   Father, we thank you;
For rest and shelter of the night,
   Father, we thank you.
For health and food, for love and friends,
   Father, we thank you.
For everything your goodness sends,
   Father, we thank you.

R.W. Emerson

Dear God, you know I'm worried about what's going to happen today. Help me to do my best and not to be upset if anything goes wrong. For Jesus' sake.   Amen.

School

Lord, thank you for all I've done today:
for new things to learn and new things to play.
Please help me to do my best each day.

Dear God, one of my friends is leaving my school:
please be with   when *he* goes to *his* new school.

Say the name of your friend.

Help *him* to be happy and to make friends quickly.

Lord, I sometimes get things wrong;
when this happens, help me not to give up,
but to try again as best I can.

Lord, tomorrow it's my first day in my new class.
Please be with me
as I get to know my new friends and my new teacher.

For reading and writing, **thank you, Lord;**
for listening and talking, **thank you, Lord;**
for singing and dancing, **thank you, Lord;**
for drawing and painting, **thank you, Lord.**　Amen.

Lord, thank you
for all the people who teach me gladly and patiently;
please help me
to learn from them gladly and patiently.

Dear God,
when someone is lonely, help me to be friendly;
when someone is upset, help me to be understanding;
when someone is angry, help me to be calm;
when someone is slow, help me to be patient;
when someone is sad, help me to be cheerful.

Dear Lord, today is the last day of the holidays, so I go back to school
tomorrow. Please help me to understand the new things which my
teachers will show me and help me to try to do my best every day.
For Jesus' sake.　Amen.

Graces

For these and all your gifts, we give you thanks, O God.

For food and fun and friendship, Lord, we give you thanks.

All good gifts around us are sent from heaven above;
Then thank the Lord, O thank the Lord, for all his love.

M. Claudius and J.M. Campbell

For every cup and plateful, Lord, make me truly grateful.

We thank you, loving Father,
for all your tender care,
for food and clothes and shelter,
and all the world so fair.

For what we are about to receive
may the Lord make us truly thankful.

Thank you, Lord, that you give us this day our daily bread.

For health and strength and daily food
we give you thanks, O God.

Bless, O Lord, the food I take,
and bless me, too, for Jesus' sake.

Bless us, O Lord,
bless our food,
bless those who made it for us,
and give food to the hungry.

Birthdays

Lord, it's been my birthday today: thank you for the fun it's been and for the people who make me happy.

A birthday is a time for giving;
giving presents shows we're friends.
God's a friend who knows and loves us;
that's a love which never ends.

Lord, it's   birthday today:

Say whose birthday it is.

Please make it an enjoyable time. For Jesus' sake.   Amen.

Happy birthday to you! Happy birthday to you!
God bless you and keep you!
Happy birthday to you!

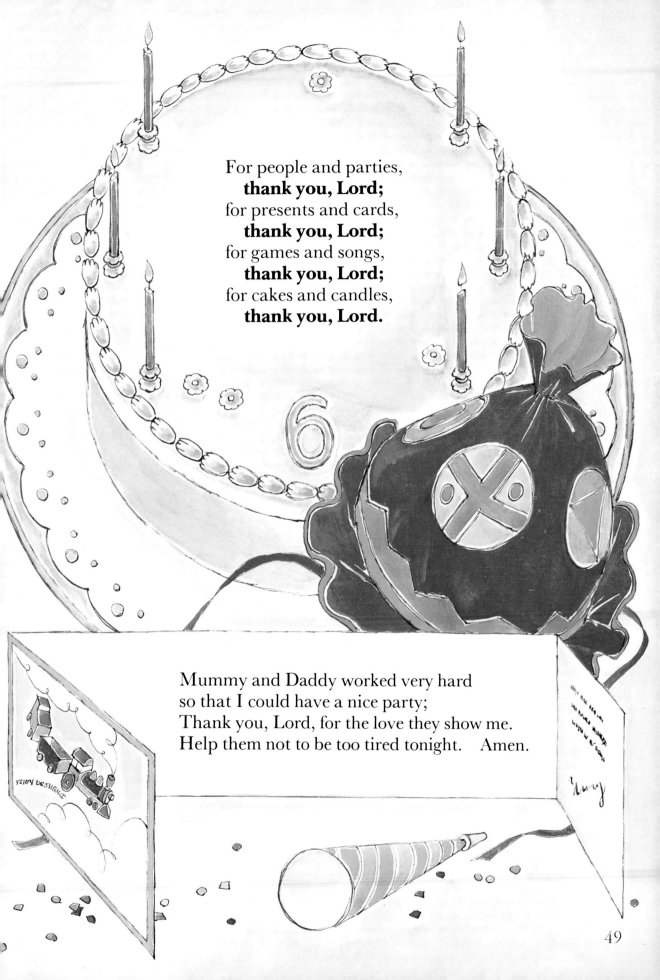

For people and parties,
thank you, Lord;
for presents and cards,
thank you, Lord;
for games and songs,
thank you, Lord;
for cakes and candles,
thank you, Lord.

Mummy and Daddy worked very hard
so that I could have a nice party;
Thank you, Lord, for the love they show me.
Help them not to be too tired tonight.   Amen.

Travelling

Dear God, be with my family and friends as they travel about, especially if they're walking or riding bikes or driving cars. Please protect them and take care of them. For Jesus' sake.   Amen.

Some travel by car, some travel by 'plane,
some travel by boat, some travel by train,
Lord, bring them safely home again.

Lord, sometimes when I have to cross a road, I'm afraid of all the cars and lorries: they're so big and make so much noise.
Help me to be careful: to obey the rules and to cross in sensible places and to make sure all is clear.

Holidays

It's holiday time again!

Lord, the grown-ups need a rest while we are away;
please help me to be thoughtful towards them every day.

Lord, thank you for this holiday,
for friends to meet and games to play.
Please keep me safe in all I do,
please make me kind and helpful too.

Lord, thank you for the seaside
and all the things I found to do.
I splashed the water and dug the sand,
I gathered shells and seaweed too.
I watched the waves as they rolled to and fro.
Where do they come from? Where do they go?
You made the water, you made the sand,
so I can be sure you'll understand.

Some prayers about Jesus

It's Christmas! It's the birthday of Jesus!
Thank you, Lord, for this happy time!

Away in a manger, no crib for a bed,
the little Lord Jesus laid down his sweet head;
the stars in the bright sky looked down where he lay,
the little Lord Jesus asleep in the hay.

The cattle are lowing, the baby awakes,
but little Lord Jesus no crying he makes.
I love you, Lord Jesus; look down from on high,
and stay by my side until morning is nigh.

Dear God, thank you for sending Jesus into our world, to tell us how much you love us. Help us to love you too, for Jesus' sake. Amen.

Mary and Joseph had to travel a long way to Bethlehem:
    thank you, God, for giving us Jesus;
the new baby was born, not in a house, but in a stable:
    thank you, God, for giving us Jesus;
shepherds and wise men came to see the baby king:
    thank you, God, for giving us Jesus.
He was the most wonderful person who has ever lived:
    thank you, God, for giving us Jesus.

For Christmas food and decorations,
    Lord, we give you thanks;
for Christmas cards and presents,
    Lord, we give you thanks.

Christmas is a time for giving!
It's fun giving presents;
it's fun making people happy with our gifts;
thank you, Lord, that Christmas is a time for giving.

Thank you, God, for the love of Jesus.
He cared for people who couldn't hear,
   thank you, God, for the love of Jesus.
He cared for people who couldn't see,
   thank you, God, for the love of Jesus.
He cared for people who were his friends,
   thank you, God, for the love of Jesus.
He cared for people who were his enemies,
   thank you, God, for the love of Jesus.
He cared for everyone he met,
   thank you, God, for the love of Jesus.
I know that he cares for me,
   thank you, God, for the love of Jesus.   Amen.

When Jesus was on the cross,
he asked one of his friends to look after his mother:
    Lord, please help me to be thoughtful like him.
When Jesus was on the cross,
he asked God to forgive his enemies:
    Lord, please help me to be loving like him.   Amen.

Thank you, God,
    that three days after Jesus died, he came alive again.
Thank you, God,
    that because Jesus is alive, he is with me all the time.
Thank you, God,
    that because Jesus is with me, I need never be afraid.

At the end of the day

For all the people who have helped me today,
  thank you, heavenly Father;
for all the friends who have talked to me today,
  thank you, heavenly Father;
for all the things I have learned today,
  thank you, heavenly Father.

Lord, we are sorry that we shouted at each other today. We didn't mean to lose our tempers – it just seemed to happen. You know that we love each other, so please help us tomorrow to be more patient and to have a happy time.   For Jesus' sake.   Amen.

Lord, today I've wasted lots of chances
to make other people happy:
    I could have helped much more at home;
    I could have tried much more at school;
    I could have talked to someone lonely;
    I could have smiled at someone sad.
Tomorrow help me to take the chances that come my way.

Thank you, dear God, for all the things we've done together today.
For   *Say what you have done.*
And for
Thank you, in Jesus' name.   Amen.

Dear God, please forgive the wrong things we have done,
as we forgive those who have done wrong things to us.

Be near me, Lord Jesus,
I ask you to stay
close by me for ever
and love me I pray.

Lord, be near, as this day ends,
to all my family and my friends.

57

At night

Glory to you, my God, this night,
for all the blessings of the light:
keep me, O keep me, King of kings,
beneath your own almighty wings.

Thomas Ken

The moon shines on throughout the night;
countless stars light up the skies;
in the wood the rabbit scurries;
in the tree the owl cries.
Lord, to think of all these wonders
fills me with surprise.

Day and night they're moving the mail,
by air and sea, by road and rail;
thank you for the people who work to sort it out,
thank you for the people who bring letters to my house.

Jesus, tender shepherd, hear me,
bless your little lamb tonight;
through the darkness please be near me;
watch my sleep till morning light.

Mary Duncan

How to pray

God is our friend. Talking to him is called 'praying'. We can talk to him about anything. If something has made us happy or excited, we can tell him; if something has made us worried or sad, we can tell him about that too.

Thank you, God
Remember to say 'thank you' to God for all the good things you enjoy.

Sorry, God
Remember to say 'sorry' to God for the wrong things you have done.

Please, God
Remember to ask God to help other people and to help you every day. If you are not sure what to pray, look at your hand. Each finger can help you to think of someone to pray for.

This is the pointing finger it reminds me to pray for my teachers and parents who show new things to me.

My middle finger is strong: this reminds me to pray for important people such as the leaders of our country.

People who are married wear their wedding ring on this finger: this reminds me to pray for everyone I love: my friends and my family.

My little finger reminds me of people who are weak: old people, sick people, hungry people.

My thumb points back at me so lastly I pray for myself.

He's got the whole world,
                    in his hand,
he's got the whole wide world,
                    in his hand,
he's got the whole world,
                    in his hand,
he's got the whole world in his hand.

61

A note from the author

I hope that both adults and children will enjoy this book. Prayer is talking and listening to God. As with any conversation with a close friend, it involves sharing everything with him: this means both the pleasant and unpleasant aspects of our lives. It involves saying 'thank you', and 'sorry', as well as 'please' to him.

Children can use this book on their own: if they can't read, the pictures can form the basis of their prayers. Far better, however, is for parents (fathers as well as mothers!) and other adults to use the book with their children. There may be times when you pray with eyes closed and hands together; but this is a book to be held, looked at, read and discussed together. Talk about the pictures. Talk about the prayers, adapting them to your own needs and making up your own.

Bedtime may be the best occasion for a family to pray together, but often it's a busy time. Would other times be better for you? What about mid-morning? What about after lunch?

Nevertheless, it is good to pray, however briefly, at the end of the day. You can talk over the events of the day, thinking of the things for which you need to be thankful or sorry. The Bible very wisely urges us never to let a day end with anger in our hearts. Bedtime is a good opportunity to say 'sorry' to one another and to God; and this involves parents too. For parents to say 'sorry' to their children and to pray about their own worries isn't seen as weakness by a child; it deepens the relationship between them.

Children enjoy rhyme, rhythmic patterns and repetition, so I have used all three extensively in the prayers. They also like joining in, and the phrases printed in different type show where they can do so. A few of the prayers are taken from hymns. If you know the melodies, you might like to sing them together.

I have not written 'Amen' after every prayer. It is not necessary to say it, but if you would prefer to, please do so. Most of the prayers are addressed to 'God' or 'Lord'; it can confuse very young children to address Jesus as well: it can seem to them that they are talking to several people. It is best to be consistent.

Through our prayers, we can involve God in everything we do – both the trivial and the important. When parents and children pray together, this not only increases their awareness of God, but it also strengthens the bond between them. By drawing closer to God, we can draw closer to one another.

Geoff Marshall-Taylor